# Emerging From the Shadows

*Written by: Scott Thomas Meyers*

Cover Design, Artwork, and Interior Graphics, Editing and Formatting by True Beginnings Publishing. To contact the publisher, please write to the address, above.

**Ordering Information**:
To order additional copies of this book, please visit Amazon, or:
https://www.createspace.com/4514028

ISBN-13: 978-0615917108
ISBN-10: 0615917100

<u>**PRINTED IN THE UNITED STATES OF AMERICA**</u>

# ~Dedication~

*I would like dedicate this book to my children whom I love and hold dear to my heart. I also would like to thank my friends who are more like family for their continued support and encouragement. They have been a blessing and an inspiration. Life is a journey and upon this journey we face many trials and tribulations it is in these times that we learn to lean on those closest to us. We all have a story to tell and we all have unique gifts to share with those with whom we come in contact with. Remember life is an adventure, Dare to dream and dare to believe.*

*I would like to add a special dedication to Bathsheba Dailey and Selina Ahnert for helping me realize my dream. Without their steadfast devotion, these dreams may have never been realized.*

# Table of Contents

# Emerging From the Shadows

The thunder rolls in the distance
Lightning thrashing the ground
Darkness hiding unspeakable terrors
Clemency is nowhere to be found

The sentence was handed down ages ago
Waiting on death row, in my own mind
The demons screech in delight
Heaven turns its head while the angels frown

Bound by this deadly prognosis
The final decree is now in
Silence now becomes the only audible sound
Exhaling, all that's left is frozen emotions

I fashioned my own prison and sealed my own cell
Walls filled with dark eerie shadows haunt my
mind
Laying in the crumpled ruins of my own emotions
I begin to drown under the weight of my tears

Scott Thomas Meyers

Countless days of sadness and unspeakable loss
Hunted by deaths greedy sinful desire
Feeling the scorching heat of hells brimstone and
fire
Lost in my contemplations, waiting to expire

Saw my body helplessly laying there
Expecting a one way flight with no return
Captivated by that shining light
In reverence standing in front of massive gates of
pearl

Should have died a long time ago
Just wasn't my time
Not even within this river of tears
There are mountains I have yet to climb

Darkness destroyed by a single flicker of light
Emerging from the shadows
My head held proudly high
I am ready to live and prepared to fight

*Emerging From the Shadows*

# Twilight's Glistening Journey

Be still thy heart and cry no more
Rise from the depths of thy fragmented ashes
It is time for you to take upon new wings and soar
To the heavens where twilight's ambiance flashes

Roam no longer in the darkness of the night
Your ghostly apparitions are not meant for the day
A mystical time now becomes your true abode
Ravenously haunted – your no longer the prey
Twilight's gleaming proves new seeds of sewed

Escape from thy night – hide thyself from the day
Neither sun nor moon shall guide thy flight
Your journey the sum of a Shakespearean play
While the of blood of black ink spills Soulfully
Twilight's glistening illuminates purely and wholly

Scott Thomas Meyers

# To Touch Love

Forever - boulevards sparsely traveled
Doubt plagues love - saneness becomes unraveled
Open your prisons - light your rescue fires
Eyes closed picture in your mind your desires

Giving your heart is a precious pleasure
Receiving love a prodigious treasure
Reach out dreams are just a heartbeat away
From this thin footpath the heart mustn't stray

Open your heart - reach out and touch love
A precious gift from the heavens above
No need to travel alone endlessly
Touching love's cords must be done breathlessly

*Emerging From the Shadows*

# My Secret Desire

I've soared with angels high in the heavens
Evoking imagery of love untold
Equated and estimated seconds
Watching in revulsion heartache unfold

Feeling the rush of the mighty whirlwind
Uncertainty can anyone be true
Fragmented proclaiming don't fall again
Falling in love is a hard task to do

Dreaming - beseeching she will come to me
Fervent tried true love my heart doth aspire
Breaking chains setting imprisoned souls free
Love and be loved - my true secret desire

Hearts blossoming like a beautiful rose
Waterfalls cascading of hope renewed
Exquisite symphonies yet to compose
No longer can these visions be subdued

Scott Thomas Meyers

# Fleshing Out Dreams

Mentions of hope as rays of light shines through
A fictional ocean floats thoughts of you
Imagery you're branded deep in my mind
Your beauty and poise my heart is resigned

Lyrics spoken instants of mirth to share
Fleshing out dreams - conceptions to declare
Crossroads await - choices now lay ahead
To journey - these words can't be left unsaid

Escaping solitude that we both feel
Ending this isolation this ordeal
No longer do you need to be afraid
Your lovely heart I wish to serenade

Assumed chance - gambling - I make this decree
Together our hearts can atlas be free

# The Rivers of Desire

Emotions flow fluidly through my head
Kindly probing my passions deep within
Beauty and longing that I feared long dead

Rivers of desires needing to be fed
Waterfalls cascading from streams once thin
Emotions flow fluidly through my head

Rarity - hanging on words thin as thread
Exploring not knowing where to begin
Beauty and longing that I feared long dead

The river - hope - her icy rocks I tread
Free falling submerged forever therein
Emotions flow fluidly through my head

Rapids of want wash through my riverbed
Treading whirlpools - exciting desires spin
Emotions flow fluidly through my head
Beauty and longing that I feared long dead

*Scott Thomas Meyers*

# Angel of Sorrow

Hyacinths, rose-blooms, and lilies
Truly a splendor for the eye to behold
The Garden of Eden a place of new birth
Where the lion lays with the lamb

Handcrafted is the picturesque landscape
As far as humanity can see
Colors painted meticulously
By the touch of the master's hand

We are all powerlessly and deviously led astray
Truths once elaborately celebrated
Becomes a revelation of mere deceptions
The depth of awareness yet to be foretold

Raped and pillaged by Hades
Dragged to the depths of the nether world
Ravishing the depths of our hearts
We allow him to steal our souls

The flowers have long since wilted
The magnificent effervescent colors
All the brilliant lively hues
Now just dismal shades of grays

Innocence and love deceitfully taken
Replaced with guilt and anguish
Fear becomes our black plague
While bitterness and anxiety now rules the day

Walls constructed painstakingly stone by stone
Surround the once vivacious garden
The ground now destitute and barren
Becoming nothing more than dried cracked clay

The angel of sorrow weeps uncontrollably
Guarding the once vibrant succulent gardens
Patiently waiting for our stony hearts
Once again to be turned into fertile clay

*Scott Thomas Meyers*

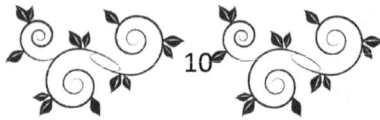

# Incensed Critique

Black velvet words spoken with forked patter.
Wait in shadow ravenous for next prey.
Dreams await, dreams they zealously shatter.
Within them, just gloom, no light, hues of grey.

Their tempter's veil cloaks black-market
knowledge.
Crouched on pedestals, prime to attack,
Love of verse, fell black ink, they acknowledge.
Drool falls from parched lips, stabbing your back.

Fanged palate ready for innocent blood,
"Criticism" they yell from honed knives.
Whitewash drowns their secret drive in flood.
Crimson stained robes hide beat-shattered lives.

Pulling at you with tattered charcoal demonic
wings,
"Advice" they proclaim as the scream of hatred
their heart sings.

*Emerging From the Shadows*

# Always Searching

Always searching - mindless thoughts dart
Loves scars forever they will smart
Yearning - for what I cannot see
Blind by dismal reality
Begging loneliness to depart

Before you lay a bleeding heart
Thirsts for a soft touch - a new start
Yen, love, and sensuality
Always searching...

Loyal to find my split apart
Final ink for my abstract art
Seeing both flesh and fantasy
Hopeful for this veracity
Never these desires shall I part
Always searching...

*Scott Thomas Meyers*

# Message in a Bottle

Dreams drifting upon the vast empty ocean
Upon this restive sea where my heart floats
Lost in the tempest of the raging cruel storms
Capsized shall I be lost- drifting for eternity

For years I have cried out to the heavens above.
Alone In the crow's nest searching for true love.
Some say I have searched hopelessly way too hard
Looking for my final refuge within the austere mist

As the sand spills slowly through hour glass
There is left but only one hope – one simple task
Through tears of I spill the blood of black satin ink
I write a secret note - anxiously done with a
heartfelt ambition

A sealed scroll with tears of blood that wax old
Placed within an empty glass bottle and sealed
tightly with a cork

*Emerging From the Shadows*

Reserved usually for those with a gloomy fate
Upon this wooded plank standing frozen
overlooking the emotional depths

Tossing my message to the angry gods of the sea
Upon this tireless journey in which my heart openly
glides
Drifting wearily - hoping to reaching the shores of a
pure heart
Opened atlas the message of my heart – In which
I'm finally found

*Scott Thomas Meyers*

# The Cycle of Life

Suppressed by fleshly dualistic fears
Bound by the dark wounds of insanity
Wounds can't heal when pain is so real
Lingering are doubts time cannot erase

Unity of life and death split into opposites
The hungry earth devourers her children
Captivated only by hopes resonating light
Shining in blackness of night expectation builds

In the depth of the moons halo like glow
Animation from the dust of the universe
Impregnates the depths of her fertile soil
From the ashes a decree of novel delivery

Harmony and destiny hear an eternal plea
Fresh planted in humanity is faiths prolific seed
Watered by the heaven's restorative rain
The cycle of life's salvation - balance to be restored

*Emerging From the Shadows*

# The Hunter

Faded lost forever in shades of gray
Carved deep within this granite stone
An epitome written for others who stray
The ravens stalk from their perched throne

Crimson ink speaks of vanities iron prison
As the hunter zealously seeks out his prey
Huntington's thirsts awakens its passion risen
All that's left –is its desolation to display

Waiting in the darkness walls silent and pale
The verdict in - no time for mourning
Inks spills carve out this vicious somatic tale
Captive waiting on the hangman's warning

Lyrical phrases flow with one true mission
Held my head up high in hopes to heal
Passing the keys of life my secret ambition
Fated and stamped with this seal

Scott Thomas Meyers

# Dreams beneath Icy Waters

Shall winters frost hide hearts for safekeeping?
Frozen deeply below the glassy pond
Hope ice- covered ~ Faith ever sleeping
Dreamscapes beseeching for warmth to respond

Snow swept visions of pure intimacy
Never to be chilled in the light of day
Ice flowers formed with pure intricacy
Glistening on a starry moonlit bay

Her enticing images beckon to me
Tempting me from the icy depths below
Enchantress of ice I beseech to thee
From crystalline flowers let your love show

Dreams of desire ravish the coldest heart
Winter's lust begs your passion to impart

*Emerging From the Shadows*

# The Hidden Garden - A Field of Dreams

There is a hidden garden of beautiful dreams
Plush Gardens where majestic flowers unfold
Insatiable  desires carry me there so it seems
Renewing my faith, restoring hope, and joy untold

Meadows of hope - to be drawn there every day
Hidden gardens - these stunning fields of dreams
Lavish beauty washes all cares and burdens away
Blooming into a reality sewn together at the seams


An new orchard of hope – God -  I pray thee
Shaded trees as I venture into the garden of love
Visions of ecstasy -  The image my heart truly sees
Gentle winds that blow through the twigs above

Begging for reality be it gardens of grass or stone
To obtain one dreams of love of my very own

*Scott Thomas Meyers*

# The Heart of God

Giving way to an era of relationship
With all my wealth that I have collected
To what ends does this fortune profit me?
If my kingdom lie in waste and hunger

I shall bestow up the beggars and serfs
The gold and jewels hidden within my coffers
From rags to riches shall be your glory
Rejoice in the splendid arches of the great hall

Sit at thy table, once reserved for the finest of
nobles
Fill thy appetite and feast upon the fatted calf
Till no longer do thy bellies hunger
A new decree to be issued sealed with my oath

Where you were once considered mere bastards
You are now sons and daughters of noble birth

*Emerging From the Shadows*

# I Can Only Imagine

Sweet, sweet dreams of unbridled passion
As I breathe in your very essence
Images of two souls entwined my mind does
fashion
The inferno of this moment knows no temperance

One Passionate kiss and I am led astray
From my depths a fire burns out of control
Restrained no longer – this fire cannot be kept at
bay
The longing in your eyes has taken its toll

I kiss your neck softly and tenderly
My tongue delightedly traces upon your skin
Methodically the intensity feeds the inferno of our
energy
Embracing we take pleasure from depths within

*Scott Thomas Meyers*

Your soft delicate curves yearning for pleasure
Our anticipation builds with every kiss
We both seek the same treasure
Our goal - sweet heavenly bliss

We become one as our bodies entwine
Moving in a magical musical tempo
The movements of our bodies methodically rhyme
Riding passionate waves until we reach the
crescendo

Spent we fall into each other's arms
Eyes lost in each other's gaze
The course of love a powerful drug that charms
I can only imagine this fiery blaze

*Emerging From the Shadows*

# Upon a Pale Horse She Rides

Upon a pale horse she gallantly rides
Deep-dyed and wove in the fabric of time
Galloping with ease across great divides

Hooves on fire riding the celestial tides
Warnings of her coming bells strangely chime
Time ever still as the scythe briskly guides

Countless times we've met as my breath subsides
Trapped in darkened silence - turned to a mime
Probing stallion eyes watch as fate decides

Life and demise feverishly collides
Blood of black ink spilled – I'll spin you my rhyme
Desolate fields - warriors choosing sides

Fatigued from battle your passion subsides
Freed from your skeletal gasp one more time
Upon angelic wings my soul resides
From this field my painted steed takes great strides

*Scott Thomas Meyers*

# *Walking in Your Shadow*

Taunted by your hellacious darkness

Walking forever in your shadow

Memories -Your cursed movie reels

Play in my mind-making me insanely blind


What the hell am I supposed to do?

I can't escape nor can I hide

Tell me why I have to feel

Laughter hiding these shards of glass


Fractured by the ultimate deception

Two hearts that never beat as one


Bold faced lies

Lost a war that could never be won!


*Emerging From the Shadows*

# I'm Not a Ghost Anymore

Once invisible to the masses

My face was nothing more than just a blur

Hiding amongst throngs - basking in my own ashes

Unlike a ghost No longer can I hide


There has always been only one true calling

Through brokenness, tears, and depths of my pain

My loss is my salvation ~ my ink is your gain

With joy I write words of empathy and healing


To leave a legacy that touches the heart chords.

Words like a beautifully played instrument

I pour out my being - it's not such a simple task -

The searing of hearts by hells double edged sword


*Scott Thomas Meyers*

Raw emotions flow from an eternal spring

Void of societies chains and the fake masks

No longer bound by the meritocracy

That torments so many lonely souls


Living amid the walking wounded feeling their pain

Frantically escaping breaking free of these chains

The fear of the unknown seizes wounded hearts.

Broke free from this vicious cycle - before it tore
my soul apart


I'd surrender everything just to live again

Not so easy from a heart that was bitterly slain.

Once haunted cowering in the darkness fearing I
was alone

Can't hide within the shadows, I'm not a ghost any
more


*Emerging From the Shadows*

# Blood Moon

With scythe in your boney hands

You feverishly slash away

Cutting to the very core

The souls you desire to reap


Gleaning the very essence of existence

Your blood lust knows no restriction

Demanding the finest specimens

Evilly you proceed upon your mission


You don the mask of a goddess

Your trappings of this world are illusory

The spirit of your mask the potential to transform

Your face of death an illusion of love and life


*Scott Thomas Meyers*

Your persona perfected by the innate desires

Of the individuals your soul seeks out to devour

Perched high on your tower you watch and wait

Your eyes seeking out your unsuspecting prey


Frost settles upon the face of the earth

The breath of life now frozen from your blue lips

The kiss of bereavement eagerly hungrily awaits

The season of the witch now in full birth

*Emerging From the Shadows*

The full moon now turns blood red

The harvest now complete

Your kiss the kiss of death

Converted by your evil powers


Lost to your hellish prowess by my own desires

Nothing left but your frail empty cracked mask

That seduced my begging soul by heavens light

And dragged me willingly into hell's fire


*Scott Thomas Meyers*

# Look Around You

Spinning out of control everything is just a blur

This world is ravenous with a hunger

Thirsting for a lasting emotion

In an ocean of tears


Do you feel the truths of what I perceive?

The wind whispers to you

As she comes closer

Caressing you with tender care


The stars hung with amazement

Shining in the blackness of night

Lighting your pathways

Turning your worrisome nights into day


*Emerging From the Shadows*

See the sun rising from the ocean

The torch of life

Illuminating our fearful souls

Sustenance on the coldest of days


Searching forever searching

The depths of these murky waters

Praying soulfully praying

For that love that makes us whole


We are one in the same - You and I

The same desires burn in our soul

A tender touch without judging

Someone who will just show they care


*Scott Thomas Meyers*

I can't be someone other than who I am

Already am what I was meant to be


Won't change who you are either

Just prove that you will be here


Maybe it's a mass delusion

No wonder we run scared

Look around you

Open your eyes we are all here

*Emerging From the Shadows*

# Reflections through the Window Pane

Through the window pane

Leaves rustle without sound

Swaying in the breeze

As summer lazily fades away


With much anticipated departure

Vanishing are the suns warm rays

As the fresh green earth makes ready

For the cool September rain


The trees ready for the morrow

Reaching their limbs to the sky

They cheerfully sing their melody

They contentedly dance in the rain


*Scott Thomas Meyers*

In the coolness of September

Eagerly they completely surrender

And ready their slumber

Vanishing are the shades of greens


With one last majestic melody

A true work of art for the eye to behold

To be displayed are their stunning colors

While they dance in the midst of the rain


*Emerging From the Shadows*

# There Still Remains an Unsung Melody

So many suffering and broken hearts

As far as the eye can see

Running away from the agony that they feel

Fearing they have nothing left on the inside


They run and they hide

Living for the faded pale memories

Mourning the wilted flowers that have died

Haunted by the shattered remains of yesterday


An army of walking wounded

Hiding in plains sight

Trembling in fear

For all the world to see


Scott Thomas Meyers

Shattered reflections of what once was

So many broken lonely people

Petrified to face tomorrow

Their head draped in indignity


The photographs and memories may fade

The rose petals may fall like dust to the earth

Sunsets will disappear into the ocean

The green grass will turn brown.


When will they open their eyes?

When will the blind see?

When will the deaf hear?

There still remains an unsung melody


*Emerging From the Shadows*

# The Seclusion of the Open Sea

Night black and dark as coal

Through the unbearable darkness

Of the midnight hour

Silence that was deafening


Through it all I have drifted endlessly

On the seclusion of the open sea

In uncharted waters

The wind unmercifully tossed me


Bound and chained to the mast

In the midst of the furious storms

Thunder crashing in the eastern skies

Lightening crackling in the dead of the night


*Scott Thomas Meyers*

The sails tattered and torn

The splintered mast laying bedsides me

The ship now badly battered

Debris clutters the raging sea


To my knees I have fallen

The angry sea hauntingly she laughs

Proclaiming victory at the sight of my vessel

Tossing me to and fro


Water now floods the hull

My soul trembles as I fear all is lost

Shattered like the splintered mast

These are remnants of broken dreams

Silently I scream

In the dead of the night

Through storms that plague my life

I dare to believe

In the darkness of midnight hour

Though my vessel is battered

The sails weathered and worn

I passionately set my course

With the breaking of the dawn

I have mastered the storm

With tears of liberation

I laugh back at the sea

*Scott Thomas Meyers*

# A Portrait That Could Never Be

Hearts broken and crippled

The wounds intentionally inflicted

Cut by a double edged sword

Words so tenderly and eagerly spoken


The crimson color now flowing

Shards bleeding lying upon the ground

Mere pieces of what once was

Broken for all to see


One left standing

While the other fallen to their knees

Hands held open

As dreams become nothing more than dust


*Emerging From the Shadows*

Sifting through trembling fingers

These are remains of what once was

Falling hopelessly to the earth

The ashes fall and turn to dust.


Clenched fist held dreams ever so tightly

Now empty palms held toward the sky

Through the remains and the ruble

I once again will arise


*Scott Thomas Meyers*

Stumbling I pick myself up

Breathing in deeply

One last look at what could have been

In this parched deserted land


Time to let go forever

Of the image I had seared into my mind

An image that never was

A portrait that could never be!


*Emerging From the Shadows*

# Screaming in silence

Alone screaming in silence

Hopes and dreams they fall

Looking to the stars for my guidance

Through the darkness I have seen it all


What was once feared I now treasure

Darkness drifts methodically toward my door

One goal, one purposes to envelope me at its
leisure

Victory within the light - darkness wishing to settle
the score


There has always been heartache and pain.

These monsters haunt me nightly in my dreams.

Misunderstood and alone this life can seem so
mundane


*Scott Thomas Meyers*

Freedom to be me - let it ring within my silent
screams


Daring to dream daring to believe

Following my heart - such a lonely road

So many lost souls looking for a reprieve

Why in the darkness have they let their dreams
erode?


Hopes and dreams expecting nothing less

than to crash and burn

Clipped your wings already you have

become grounded in your plight

Life has you believing this is a one-way

street forgetting there is always a U-turn


*Emerging From the Shadows*

Feeling like you can't face the day than rise

with me and soar into the night.


Alone screaming in the silence looking for relief

In the darkness I know there are others

who share my plight.

Lift me up and I will fly away shedding this disbelief

Why do we cower alone when there are so

many to stand together and fight?

*Scott Thomas Meyers*

# Love

Love is unconditional and is blind.

Love doesn't proclaim, I don't have the time.

Love is patient, long suffering, gentle, and kind.

Love is not full of anger, nor is it resentful

all the time.

True love believes that better times

always lie ahead.

Love is bound by a bond that is an

unbreakable thread.

Love does not venture outside the fold;

Love does not look at its mate and think

that this is getting old.

Love looks deep into the eyes of their mate.

Love sees the glory, the glow, and beauty

of their mate

*Emerging From the Shadows*

When the sparkle is gone from the eyes

of the one you love.

It is time to question what went wrong,

and pray to the heavens above.

Love will desire and fight for what

one truly believes.

When everyone else questions, love will defend

what no one else is willing to see.

Love is the one thing we all truly desire.

It is the one thing that motivates and

sets our hearts afire.

There is a difference between lust and love.

One last for fleeting moment the other blessed

from God above.

*Scott Thomas Meyers*

# Secret Note

I sit here with much emotion and ambition to

write a secret note

It is dreams upon the ocean for which my heart

will always float.


For years I have cried out to God above.

Seeking and searching for nothing but true love.


Some say I have searched and tried to way to hard.

A broken vessel, with walls built so high,

that now only I see through the bars.


Tears still flow freely, which I thought over

time would dry up and dissipate.


*Emerging From the Shadows*

I know with my story and these raw emotions

most of you truly can relate.


Why is it we have come sadly to expect this of

our life's story.

Believing our dreams will lay deeply buried

for eternity, within a rocky quarry.


So I sit here and write a secret note ~ it's done

with a heartfelt ambition.

Pick up your broken shards ~ dare to dream ~ dare

to believe ~ watch your dreams come into fruition.


*Scott Thomas Meyers*

Fear not anymore, with resolution and

commitment, dive deep into that rocky quarry.

Look truly for your heart's desire, if we do not then

in the end, sadness will be your life's story.


I sit here with ambition, with a passion and fervor
unmatched; to you write a secret note.

Like lilies in the water once they are in full bloom,
let your dreams once again be set afloat.

*Emerging From the Shadows*

## Dare to Dream

The sun blotted out the sky dark black as coal.

A heart imprisoned, like words painstakingly sealed

on a waxy scroll.


Seems as fate has charted it tedious course!

From faith, hope, and dreams it issues a deathly
divorce.


The sounds of the shackles clanging bitterly on the

cold damp floor.

Into the darkness of the night freedom lies beyond

that cell door.


Chained by the fetters that bind ones soul!


*Scott Thomas Meyers*

Heartache and doubt now seems to have

taken their toll.

Demonic powers eerily screech in delight

The angelic host issues a decree for you

to stand and fight.

Stand in the midst of this raging conflagration!

Remember your dreams!

They are the cornerstone of your Foundation.

Fight you ask - when all hope seems lost?

Stand and fight I say - count the cost!

What will it profit you to lose your soul?

Why allow heartache and misery to take their toll?

*Emerging From the Shadows*

Yes I say - stand and face this black plague

that would rob your soul!

Dream not, and be counted amongst the lost –

as the Angel of death rings the bells last toll.


Beyond the self-imposed prison walls of your heart,

Lays a beautiful palate, of brilliant colors for you to

dream a work of art.


The keys of freedom lie within your grasp.

The chain that carries them, bound by forgotten

dreams - such a flimsy clasp.


Freedom lies within your power,

Even while in the dark corners you cower.

Remember who you are and what you truly desire.

Dare to dream and you'll quench hell's fire.


*Scott Thomas Meyers*

# Would You Save My Soul

Would you save my soul?

Would you touch my heart and make it whole?

Will you look into my eyes?

Will you wipe away the tears that I cry?

Would you truly love me?

Would you allow me to be all that I desire to be?

Would you be willing to take away all the pain?

Walk hand in hand with me in the midst

of the rain?

Would you walk with me along life's
celestial shore?

Allowing our hearts to the heavens to soar?

Kissing softly and oh so tenderly.

Giving of yourself wholeheartedly.

Will you open your heart?

**Emerging From the Shadows**

Loving completely never to be torn apart?

In return I offer to you -

A love complete - a love so true,

The heat of passion and tender romance.

In your eyes I would forever be lost in a trance.

Undeniable and unconditional love.

Together we would soar to the heavens above.

Would you save my soul?

Be willing to love completely and allow our hearts

the heavens to patrol?

*Scott Thomas Meyers*

## As Strong as I Can Be

Words unspoken somewhat out of fear!

Trying so hard to believe that someone can care!

Lost in this fog and the coolness of the night air!

Seemingly forever I have been trapped within

this living nightmare.

A picture of strength is what I try to convey.

Waiting for the darkness of this night to turn into

a brighter day.

The truth is it's more like abstract art.

Twisted, painful, and lonely is the portrait of my heart.

*Emerging From the Shadows*

Longing and desire fill my soul.

Make me believe that my torn heart can

be made whole.


As strong as I can be

That's what is expected of me.


Can you hear the words that I cannot speak?

Shall you judge shall you critique?


Let thy scales fall from thy eyes.

Look in my heart it will tell you no lies.


Raw emotions full of fear hurt and pain.

Will these truths your opinion of me stain?


*Scott Thomas Meyers*

Sympathy is not what I desire.

True love, and friendship, the gifts I wish

to acquire.


While the pain and loneliness fill me heart.

The truth is that love and honesty prevail

they have from the very start.


In the midst of this fiery trial -

I still look for and believe in all that's worthwhile.


As strong as I can be

That's what am ~ that's what I believe


*Emerging From the Shadows*

# All Hopes Now Rest Upon the Rising Sun

In all the majesty and colors of the setting sun!

Another day has ended and new night has begun.


The darkness creeps into every corner.

Left there with another hapless ending like

a spiteful mourner


The eerie emptiness and loneliness steals ones
soul.

Falling deeper and deeper into this black hole!


The hopes and dreams of that day all but

washed all away.

Feeling lost and lonely I'm like a dreadful stray.


*Scott Thomas Meyers*

The midnight hours unmercifully takes their toll -

In this damp darkness black as coal!


Alone and empty - seems like a void in time

and space.

Fretfully - pondering all the steps needing

to retrace.


The quest through the darkness is well on its way.

This beast lurking in the shadows

I must become victorious and slay.


All hopes now rest upon the rising sun.

Another night has ended and new day has begun.


*Emerging From the Shadows*

# Through the Troubled Waters

Through the troubled waters I must travel,

Along life's shores

where dreams are left broken and shattered.


As the temptress billows crash into the shore,

These uncharted waters I must now explore.


The beauty lies not only upon the still of the

waters,

It lays the treasure of dreams locked in our coffers.


Into the depths of the murky ocean I must dive

To see the true beauty that's hidden yet, surreal

and alive.


*Scott Thomas Meyers*

In the midst of the fierce and raging storm.

To complicity of complacency - I must not conform.


Conform you scream! – To what? - What society

sees as a norm?

Along the rocky beaches of broken hearts

and dreams?

No sir I wish not to conform!


Drifting along the horizon my vessel does explore.

No longer my heart and dreams can I ignore.


*Emerging From the Shadows*

# In My Dreams

In my dreams she loves me.

She is my eyes when I can no longer see.

Her love is setting me free.

In my heart of hearts she loves me.


Her eyes capture the entire colors of the rainbow,

Her smile radiates all of the different hues.

From lips sweat as honey words of

endearment flow

Her love turns the gray skies blue.


Like the dawn breaking through and turning

night into day.

She believes in me even when all others

tend to stray.

*Scott Thomas Meyers*

She is loving me, her heart always knows the

right words to say.

In my dreams she loves me,

this I truly pray.


To open my heart, her tenderness won't quit ~

her heart will continually try.

Her heart reaches out with love and rescues me

She will reach in and her love will give

my heart wings to once again fly.

In my dreams she loves me.

*Emerging From the Shadows*

# Now You and I Can be freed

Skies turn black - as the sun is blotted out

Death seems to have become the victor

As mankind's depravity spins out of control

Rage like a wildfire consumes the heart of man

With a lust for blood we do hunger

Who are, we and what have we become?

With malice we act, and as violent crowd

we become one

With anger and hatred seething from our pours

We scream for justice and demand the

price be paid

Justice for love, grace, healing, and mercy

The price should be nothing less than death

*Scott Thomas Meyers*

Who does he think he is to spread?

A message of hope!

We'll show him, aren't we the ones in control?

To try to take that from us would be futile

We shall fight to gain independence

Revolt, rise up and riot

We will fight God if we can

Death to the Savior

Or is it death to man?

OH death where is they victory

OH grave where is they sting

He rose three days latter

Now you and I can be freed

# Her First Kiss

Her eyes crystal clear as the sea

Looking into them I was lost, careless, and free.


A smile that could warm the coldest heart

Seeing her I desired her from the start.


Her touch would send shivers through my spine

This touch is the touch

I have desired for all of time.


Her laughter was spontaneous and full of delight.

With broken wings my heart began to take flight.


*Scott Thomas Meyers*

Like the honeysuckle in the springtime

Her lips were sweet and tender

and just as delicate and fine.


I was graced by her beauty and poise.

Time spent with her one of my greatest joys.


I was lost in heavenly bliss,

The very moment I felt her first kiss.


*Emerging From the Shadows*

# Oh What a Tangled Web is Weaved

Oh what a tangled web is weaved

When in our hearts we live in doubts believed.

Is it so hard to speak and believe in the truth?

We long for the love we dreamed of as youth.

Loneliness is a hard path to escape.

When behind these walls our hearts

have been raped.


Accustomed to the darkness of the midnight hours,

We dare to dream from our

keeps and prison towers.


*Scott Thomas Meyers*

Thoughts racing endlessly through our mind,

Craving love and searching for the sanity that we can't seem to find.


Keys for our freedom jingle at the door.

Yet we cower in the dark recesses and

corners on the coldness of the floor.

Oh what a tangled web is weaved

When in our hearts we live in doubts believed.

*Emerging From the Shadows*

# Reach Out for Me

Made my mistakes I'm just a man

There is no price I wouldn't pay

An image in my own mind

Look deeply in my eyes

They burn with an inferno of fire

Desire that drives me crazy

Drowning in the depths of this flood

Hearing the whispers in the dark

Tired of old memories

Reach out for me

Nothing left inside to hide

Nothing but some feelings

That I have missed the best part of love

Searching no more

Of a love worth dying for

*Scott Thomas Meyers*

Busting out of these chains

The prisoner I once was

I am determined to be set free

Walls have come crashing down

I have fallen to me knees

Reach out for me

Nothing left inside to hide

Nothing but some feelings

That I have missed the best part of love

I need someone to truly show me

Of a love not forsaken

Tell me I can't be too late

Riding this storm out till the end

Even if forever I drift endlessly

In my heart I can't give up hope

I have no choice but to always believe

*Emerging From the Shadows*

# *If Only to Believe*

If only to believe...

A seed planted and conceived.


A new hope to be born,

From this heart that has been torn.


To trust yet again a desire deep within

Just have to break through this hardened skin.


To reach into my heart and make me believe.

See through my eyes touch my soul,

help me receive.


A desire lies deep within my surface.

That burns hotter than a kiln or furnace.


*Scott Thomas Meyers*

Haven't given up my dreams,

I pray it comes just like others so it seems.


Have I made it thus far in life –

I question is it too late.

Will this crooked path

I walk ever be made straight?


Can you feel my heart beating

do you hear its beckon call?

Will someone reach out their hand

before lose hope and fall?


If only to believe that there is something left for me


*Emerging From the Shadows*

Likened to the quest for the Holy Grail –

I just want to see.


Reflecting on my life's choices,

Calling out for hope waiting to hear the voices


There has to something left - just have to believe.

One day what I truly seek I may just receive


If only to Believe...


*Scott Thomas Meyers*

# I Question Why

*Dedicated To Sandi Dunbar:*

*In Memory of Justin CupcakeTowle*

There is an unbearable pain deep within my heart.

Your loss is devastating and tearing me apart.


I never even had a chance to see you and

say my goodbye.

You drove away that stormy morning –

who knew you would die.


The tears that flow freely are like a waterfall.

As I lay here daily upon my pillow my

tears they do fall.


*Emerging From the Shadows*

You were more than a brother you were my

best friend.

I always knew I could count on you until

the very end.


I look to the heavens and continually question why.

All I can do now is hope you're watching me

from that blue sky.


There is not a passing moment that you are

not in my thoughts.

Even after all the battles as brother and sister

that we fought.


They say that with time the heart will heal.

How can that be when with your sudden passing I
cannot possibly deal?


*Scott Thomas Meyers*

Pictures of you like a movie play through my

head night and day.

This heartache and your loss on my soul and

heart they do weigh.


A tragedy like this is supposed to make us stronger.

The truth be told, there are times I feel as if

I can't go on any longer.


You are gone unfairly and at such a young age.

Why did you leave me and how do I

turn a new page.


Yes of course,

question and ask God continually why.

Is there a bigger plan for you?

Or did he just want you by his side.


*Emerging From the Shadows*

I am I being selfish as to not wanting to lose

you or to let go?

No little brother I will always hold on and

cherish your memory though.

I wander through this life daily and go

about my routine.

I truly miss the times now when

I was able to count on you - to me your loss
is obscene.

I ask myself this question, what I to do am

and to who do I turn to now

Friends and family are there,

but to your memory my loyalty I vow.

I love you little brother visions of you still

dance in my head and in my heart.

I can make you this one promise though even

with your passing we are never far apart.


*Scott Thomas Meyers*

# The Dark Side of the Rainbow

*Dedicated to a dear Friend Joseph*

There is a darkness that clouds over my soul.

My life has been lived with pride and yet

self-control.


I have chosen a path that is different than

many others.

The symbol of the rainbow I travel with the

masses of numbers.


This is supposed to be an acceptant society.

However my life is filled with pain and anxiety.


*Emerging From the Shadows*

I sit here alone with the darkness that clouds

my rainbow.

Like a contestant on some sort of weird

game show.


I have had a few friends that have stood

by my side.

It was them who made me stand up in my

turmoil and still have my pride.


The others have led me down the wrong path

now I am lost lonely and astray.

I am not worthy of the normal peoples glances,

I wonder where is acceptance - maybe someday.


*Scott Thomas Meyers*

The rainbow has always stood for hope joy

and peaceful tomorrows.

However I live on the dark-side of the

rainbow - filled with nothing but pain and sorrow.


To others I'm joyous and smile yet as

I lay awake at night I admit I am lost.

If there are truly so many of us why are then

why are we still paying high the cost.


What society sees as deviant and

truly quite unique?

Our lives are lost and alone and at the

most very often bleak.


I desire no more than you or the person standing

in the street.


*Emerging From the Shadows*

A love that is true,

everlasting a heart like you desire that is unique.


I have traveled down the wrong path to

hide my pain.

You laugh at me,

while I scream inside and try not to go insane.

What will it take for you to view me as an

individual with the respect that I deserve?

To hold my head up high I truly desire –

when you see my lifestyle choices and as you
watch and

observe.

The rainbow has always stood for hope joy

and peaceful tomorrows.

I live on the dark-side of the rainbow –

hoping for peaceful, loving tomorrows.


*Scott Thomas Meyers*

# Secrets on a Closet Shelf

As the days go by I want to be able to always

look myself straight in the eye.

I have to live with myself as walk outside and as

I look to the sky.


I don't want to stare at the setting sun.

And hate myself for the things I have done.


I don't want to keep secrets about myself

on a closet shelf.

I want to be happy with the life choices

I have made for myself.


**Emerging From the Shadows**

I fool myself into thinking that no one else

will ever know.

The kind of girl I really am, yes I am afraid it

will truly show.


I don't want my mind to let me breakdown

into my shame.

I want to go all out with my head held high –

to me this is no game.


I truly want to deserve all the other girls respect.

If they truly knew who I was –

what image would it project?


But there is this struggle from deep within

for acceptance and popularity.


*Scott Thomas Meyers*

Who I am now is far from acceptable

and considered a rarity.

I don't want to keep secrets about

myself on a closet shelf.

I want to be happy with the choices

I have made for myself.


I have a deep desire to be able to look in the

mirror and like myself

In these days with the choices I have made

it's hard to face one-self.


At least I can say that I am not a fake, or a bluff.

As I try and try again, I can never seem to hide

from myself and all of this stuff.


*Emerging From the Shadows*

I see what others may never see,

and know what others may never know.

Hopefully in time when a woman I become my

lifestyle choices, peoples hatred will outgrow.


It truly seems that I can never fool myself,

so whatever happens; I want to be conscience free,

Self-respecting as well as respected –

the woman I should have always been

allowed to be.

*Scott Thomas Meyers*

# Slow fade

There is a slow fade that has been taking

place deep with in my heart.

This fade I prayed would be blocked and

would not happen from the start.


Time has a way of washing away the hurts

and the pain

As the waves roll in it washes away the love that

I once was able to sustain.


The words you speak come easy to you.

Hoping I will once again believe and

be made the fool.


*Emerging From the Shadows*

A slow fade over time has been taking place.

I have searched my heart and now the pain

has begun to erase.


Months and months have passed as

I held on to a simple promise.

All the while your words were empty –

you were so heartless.


I wanted and deserved to be firsts in your life –

you think I can be your second or third choice.

I screamed from my heart you were

my heart's desire -

and you still refused to listen to my voice.


I spoke to with words of adoration,

devotion, and, of love.


*Scott Thomas Meyers*

I so desired to be the man that you looked at

and would be proud of.


I wanted you to look deep into my eyes.

You would have seen a heart devoted solely

to you with bonds that ties.


Still to this day you tell me words you think

I want to hear.

If love was truly your plan you would

have somehow shown me you cared.


It is not enough for a simple phone once in a

blue moon.

I felt as if my heart was hit and destroyed

by a typhoon.


*Emerging From the Shadows*

You speak those three words - that are supposed

to come from the heart.

With every second that passes a feel the slow

fade pulling us farther and farther apart.


You left that eventful day with no goodbyes

or words that were spoken

No explanation was given in the months

to come my heart was utterly broken.


The slow fade away has been taking place all along.

I asked you to prove your heart I guess

I still believed and I was wrong.


To you this may seem like some sort of game.

And I truly loved you –

all I can proclaim is what a shame.


*Scott Thomas Meyers*

The truth is known I would have loved you

completely and forever.

It was my goal when the vows were said and as we

set out on our endeavor.


There is a slow fade that has been taking place

deep with in my heart.

This fade I prayed would be blocked and would not

happen from the start.

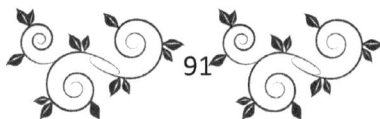

# Memories

### Written for Patricia Briehof Harvey

Memories are pictures in our heart and head that

we hope do not fade with the sands of time.

Memories of a life together, a family created our

journey together and the mountains we climbed.


You were my confident, my lover, and best friend,

and all that I truly knew.

We were bound together by the unbroken chains

of true love - this gift is reserved for a select few.


Our Life together was everything I could have

hoped for or dreamed more than I had planned.

It was a love story for all to see, in all our glory, our

children - our lives together were grand.

*Scott Thomas Meyers*

Still nightly the images of you dance in my head.

As lay here sobbing quietly in my bed.


You were here one second and gone the next –

without even a chance to say goodbye.

As I looked around our home all I could truly see

was your face -tears streaming down my face as

I cried.


The empire we built together came crashing to

the ground.

I had to pick myself up, and a desire for a new

hope had to be found.

*Emerging From the Shadows*

Life changing choices would have to make- without

the aid off my confident, my lover, and my friend.

The loss would be great and at times my own

personal hell I would have to descend


The memories of your voice haunted me

everywhere went and wherever I was –

my love you truly were my best-friend.

I knew that if I was to make through this loss

I would have but one choice this mountain

I would have to climb and transcend.


You left me a precious gift though and a story

to be told.

You are everywhere as

I see the beauty of the roses unfold.


*Scott Thomas Meyers*

To me each rose has a special meaning

and is a gift from the heavens above.

It is as if you are looking down and still

showing me your guidance and your love.


Memories are pictures in our heart

and head that we hope do not fade with the sands

of time.

Your legacy lives on in my heart, the life we shared,

our children we had, and the mountains we

climbed.


Time has passed and the memories still do not

fade.

However I look to the rose and am no longer afraid.


*Emerging From the Shadows*

## Innocent Desire's

There is a fire that burns it's an innocent desire.

The fire that burns for you I prayed would

transpire.

You and I had dreams that never came to be.

It's as if these desires were thrown into the

deep blue sea.

A love that would cool in the middle of the night

Like the fire as it cooled it lost its flaming light.

An innocent desire to see a true love through -

Tell me that true love could not be so untrue.

*Scott Thomas Meyers*

Innocent desires are dreams born deep

within the heart.

They give two souls a desire for hope and a

fresh start.


Tell me that these dreams are more than

a mere desire.

Within the still of night they were born inside

of me - a new fire.


An Innocent desire It is a wonder

we made it this far.

Tell me these goodbyes won't leave yet

another scar.

Is there still hope for innocent desires?

Fires that will burn once again and transpire!


*Emerging From the Shadows*

# On The Open Sea

I drift endlessly upon the cold dark waters

of the open sea.

I fear that this cold harsh water will be my demise -

many of you disagree.


Through the darkness of the long gloomy nights.

I am lost feeling like I have lost all of my own rights.


The storms have come and gone and

have taken their toll.

I look into the distance for a glimmer of hope;

still I drift endlessly with no control.


*Scott Thomas Meyers*

I study the horizon looking for that

Shimmering light.

For my safety against these rocky shoals –

I pray fervently about my plight.


Still the raging seas they wash over me endlessly,

I float here gasping for breath.

Uncertain of my personal storms there are times

that I must admit I have prayed for death.


I am drifting lost and lonely on this merciful,

bone chilling, endless sea.

My dreams have been crushed and soon my

demise will follow - the question is to what degree.

These are the storms I face as

I drift endlessly, upon the cold murky

waters of that open sea.

My only hope is to see a vision in the distance of

the night, a light that flashes bright setting me
free.


There is but one hope when we face these

harsh angry seas.

Look up to the heavens for there is but only who

one can calm the storms and set us free.


*Scott Thomas Meyers*

# Is anybody Out There

Is there anybody out there?

I cry out but no one can hear me I fear.


My heart has been wrapped in these chains.

In bondage I have lived, I am racking my brains.


Why must I live in this sea of faces?

Lost among the throngs –

drifting to different places.


Tell me as I walk against the grain.

Is there anyone who can set me free - break this chain.


*Emerging From the Shadows*

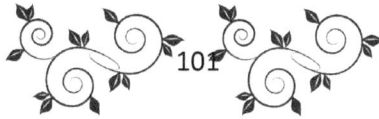

Can a person be so lost unable to receive love?

Must I remain a captive am I truly that

unworthy of?


How is one truly supposed to believe?

It wasn't always this way I once was able to receive.


Now I admit that I am lost in the darkness

I am overtaken by the pain and the harshness.


Is there anybody out there?

Can you feel my pain can you truly hear.


Darkness turns light, yet another dawn has brought
a new day.


*Scott Thomas Meyers*

Again I find myself in the ashes crying

again in the rain.


In my heart I feel the chains as they wrap

around my heart squeezing so tight.

I have to admit I stand against the storms yet

alone I seem to stand and fight.


How long will my heart be held captive?

Why has God made my spirit so loving and passive?


I now stand screaming is there anybody out there?

Begging but no one can hear me I fear.


Tell me in this world I am not alone.

If not then plant a seed and let it be sown.


*Emerging From the Shadows*

Let hope arise from the dust and the ashes.

Before loneliness and love in this world clashes.


Amongst the millions of people I cannot be the

only one.

I try to over and over to escape but the pain

I cannot outrun.


Is there anybody out there?

I cry out but no one can hear me I fear.


*Scott Thomas Meyers*

# Voices in My Head

There are voices constantly in my head

They whisper in the darkness,

I'm hanging by a thread.


The hang man has come with my chains that

bind me

Placed the noose around my neck,

I cry loudly one last time to be free


My shame hasn't always been this way,

For years I followed the path and then

led was astray.


The voices whisper to me in the midnight hours.


*Emerging From the Shadows*

I am void of strength - chained I have no powers.

I've relinquished all rights now the voices

of the dark ones call me.

Every night I scream out in pain, begging,

doesn't anyone here my plea?


I must live with my past mistakes, the losses

far outweighs than the gains.

The voices in my head are calling out to remind

me of my sins and their stains.


Every night there are voices in my head;

there is a fight for my life and my body.

The dark ones come for me, however the angels

and God grace my soul and now they do embody.


*Scott Thomas Meyers*

I am overwhelmed by the beauty

and realize that shame can no longer be

In the midst of the voices calling out,

I am reminded that from the cross I was set free.


The chains that bound me fall freely from

around me, what was stolen from me will be
replaced.

When I cry out in the midnight hours,

I now call out a new name, and in his presence I'm
Graced.

The voices in my head are no longer from the

dark images that I see.

The voices are from heavenly beings,

as I can now claim I have been set free.


*Emerging From the Shadows*

# Obscurity

Let me pose a question to you as you

journey through this life in obscurity.

Have you ever felt the lack of importance –

a lack of complete surety?


Have you ever felt like you were invisible?

To those around you

The pain that you carry in your heart is

misunderstood and only felt by a few.


Thoughts plague your heart, you doubt your
purpose of being,

and troubling thoughts fill you mind.


*Scott Thomas Meyers*

It is if no one understands what you are feeling,
and the death warrant has already been signed.


To feel obscure is like the clouds moved in and

covered the sun from illuminating the sky.

Darkness haunts the soul day and night, you can't

escape the emotions no matter hard you try.


To walk in obscurity is to walk with your head hung

low, you're afraid someone might see deep into

your soul.

Your failures and transgressions, written on a

parched piece of paper - waiting to be read for

everyone to know.


*Emerging From the Shadows*

Obscurity is daunting task to hide from,

as you walk in complete fear.

The fear is to be found out and

still feel like no one truly understands or truly
cares.


As you journey through this life in obscurity realize

that those around you are walking the same path.

hiding from those around them they have but one

purpose, and that is to hide their eyes and avoid

the same wrath.

*Scott Thomas Meyers*

# The Journey

Ages ago in a mystic time and place -

I was entered into a long winding dangerous race.


The task that was set before me.

Were challenges that I could not foresee.


In the darkest recesses my mind.

The purpose Gods has kept my eyes blind.


The journey has now spanned decades of time.

Still I have no idea his purpose I cannot find.


With no control the quest has been

mapped out before me.


*Emerging From the Shadows*

My mind and my body from pain they cry

out continually to be free.


It is always with a broken spirit and

a shattered heart, and a heavy laden soul.

I cry out dear God please

I want to be free from the cross I must bear let me
go.


This cry, this heart felt plea, on deaf ears it

does not fall.

His purpose - with my words –

to touch one and inspire all.


So now fervently with emotion

I must write down these words in this time and
place.


*Scott Thomas Meyers*

With all my heart and soul, a shattered, broken

man, I must with all I have finish this race.


I reach out to all who are willing to read the words

set before them.

For we who have a broken heart and are heavy

laden, are truly his gems.


So with a broken body, while I travel this journey it

is with heart love

That I beg of you not to look at me, but to see his

unconditional love


*Emerging From the Shadows*

# A Place Called Home

I desperately long for a place that I can call Home.

It is a place where I belong; no longer will

my soul roam.


I admit freely that I have wandered so far away.

That the heavy burdens and sadness on

my heart do weigh.


I long for family that will always

be there to love and relate.

Or to a love with a pureness to which

I can honestly say was fate.


*Scott Thomas Meyers*

A Place called home,

I long with my heart and soul to be.

I have seen the glory and

I pray finally from pain to be set free.


A place called home is something that is

just made for me.

It is filled with happiness and joy;

yes from my heartache I will be free.


A place called home one of my own

that is my shelter.

I now know the only way there is to

kneel at his holy alter.


*Emerging From the Shadows*

I have lost my place in this world I have looked for

a place called home

So with these few words I must admit that my body

is only here on loan.


I long for a place called home a place where I can

say I truly belong.

I desire a new hope in my heart with a love that

never fails, so be it I crave a new song.


*Scott Thomas Meyers*

# I Cry Out

My heart is screaming and I cry out

I look for my meaning, what is my life about.


I admit freely I have lost my place in this world.

My emotions like paint on a canvas are all swirled.


I cry out from the very core of my soul.

Show me my path before death takes its toll.


I cry out to thee in the heavens above.

I cry out to you, with a labor of love.


I cry out to find meaning, love, hope, and purpose.


*Emerging From the Shadows*

Only with your design may I find my way,

for it is your compass.

I cry out to thee with hope and a new resolution,

That from the darkness, I will find

complete absolution.

I cry out to thee - nightly, seeking and listen for

your answer from above

I cry out and not knowing where else to turn,

knowing from this pain I am tired of.

*Scott Thomas Meyers*

# The Man in the Mirror

Who is this man starring back at me the man that

I now see?

The man looking through a shattered mirror

could this truly be?


I see distorted broken images of the man

I once was.

Mistaken thoughts and raw emotions are

the probable clause.


The man in the mirror sees many images of

who he has become.


*Emerging From the Shadows*

To be honest his loss and brokenness,

and broken dreams he has succumb.


Shattered images stare back at him;

he knows not which is truly him.

His past, present, and future,

to him the look bleak and pretty grim.


A restless heart my thoughts are turning my

pain constantly churning.

Still to this shattered image of a man

staring back there is a fire burning.


Desires for the shattered reflections once

again to be made whole.


*Scott Thomas Meyers*

I would lay down my life and this very night to you give my soul.


The man in the mirror is always starring back at

me with shattered reflections

A deep desire burns from within to be proud of

myself and leave a whole pure reflection


Yes I am the man in the mirror starring at shattered

images anything different a change this would be.

I long for wholeness, a deep desire from the very

depths, to look just once and see a whole new me.


*Emerging From the Shadows*

# The Darkness of the Night

It is in the still of the night when everyone

else is asleep.

We feel our heartache and the tears flow down

our cheeks.


It is in the darkness of the night that we wrestle

deep within our soul.

It is in this darkness our emotions are swallowed

up by a black hole.


In the light we wear a mask we smile intently as we

go about our tasks.


*Scott Thomas Meyers*

Yet when we look into our shattered mirror we

know its shallow and just a mask.


In the darkness of the night in pain and turmoil I

must face the demons of my life.

In the darkness their evil desire is to carve my heart

to pieces with the sharpest and evilest of knifes


You cannot escape no matter how hard you try the

loss and the mistakes of your past.

All you can hope for is the darkness of the night

you survive and the evil you can outlast.


*Emerging From the Shadows*

# Tears

Tears fall from my eyes like a river flows into

the ocean.

Hope, faith, and love,, is it all just a fairy tale

or just a  simple notion?


Tears when they fall are supposed to be

cleansing and set the soul free.

Like ripples in the water they grow bigger

and bigger just wait and watch you will see.


Tears they fall freely and continually from my eyes.

They have brought me low and have

destroyed my highs.


*Scott Thomas Meyers*

Tears soak my pillow in the midnight hours as

I fight this fight, for what I do not know.

My soul cries out as my body and heart is broken

I still don't know how to let go.


While it is true, my heart is saddened the tears

still flow freely like a river to the ocean

The healing if it will happen seems like

the tears that freely from my eyes happen

to flow in slow motion.

*Emerging From the Shadows*

# The Girl I Once Knew

Is this the girl I once knew to be?

A candle in the wind her flame burns bright.

Love and dedication for the entire world to see -

If I had the chance I would take her and hold in my

arms so tight.


A first love through an eternity she has held on to

Now after countless years as it seems fate has

brought her back to me

If I could have admitted then what I knew in my

heart to be true

Life's story would have been truly different you

would see.


*Scott Thomas Meyers*

Is this a cruel and cunning twist of fate -

To love, to desire, to cherish, and to truly need!

At this moment and in this time and this place!

You can't tell me I am to late

My heart and soul cry out to thee and in her love

I know I'd finally be freed.


She has a faith tested; it has been tried, and is true

I long for a woman who will walk with me down

that long, dark, narrow path.

If this be the girl I once knew, our love through the

ages of time would carry us through.

If this but a cruel a cruel twist of fate then what

have I done to feel this wrath.


*Emerging From the Shadows*

If this be the Girl That I once knew.

I cannot let go, I have to hold on, and I refuse to lose again.

An age old flame burns fervently and hot, this only

happens to a select few.

To lose this love and let the fire die, would bring unspeakable heartache, and unbearable shame.


Yes this is the girl I once knew.

To hear your voice and

still to this day feel your love.

Love can surpass the test of time,

and will always show itself true.

Now like fate I must wait in you for

passion and romance and true love.


*Scott Thomas Meyers*

# A Prisoner of My Own Devise

I gave all of myself so completely.

This wasn't done falsely or discretely.


I have become a prisoner behind my own walls

I have fought many fights and I have

lost many brawls.


Still in the darkness, I write words of wisdom or so

I thought.

Hoping to find reason and sanity for all

the battles that I have fought.


I find that I hide behind these walls

not to remember but to forget.


*Emerging From the Shadows*

I have walked in loss, head hung low, defeated with

shame I now live in regret.


I have to proclaim that I have become a prisoner of

my own devise.

There is nothing no one can offer not even the best

of advice.


For you see when one is defeated in battle he is

utterly cut off and becomes a captive.

Behind his walls a prisoner of his own devises, his

heart and soul now become adaptive.


*Scott Thomas Meyers*

# A Tender Touch

A tender caress and loving touch

I remember how it meant so much


The feelings are still there today

Romance played out as Shakespearian play


A sweet forbidden loving embrace

I remember the smile upon your face


A kiss that was tender yet so deep

Was only meant for us, our secret to keep


How can something be so wrong?

When in our hearts was created a new song


*Emerging From the Shadows*

That first tender kiss and that loving trace

Burns eternally in me now, with passion, whenever

I see your face

A passion that was as deep as it could get

Never would our two hearts be able to forget

Love is never for a fleeting moment

It will give itself away in complete abandonment

Afraid to admit what was in our hearts

We were lost in the moment from the very start


Three words felt however rarely spoken

Left our hearts lost and completely broken

A new spark starts to flourish

It is up to us and God to truly nourish.


*Scott Thomas Meyers*

Scott was born April 21 1965 in Syracuse New York, currently he is residing in New Hampshire. Writing is his way of expressing himself in hopes to reach others. Scott writes of his personal battles between the light and darkness, and love and loss, he has battled a chronic illness for the past thirteen years. His words are his legacy, his gift to give back to those who are fighting their own battles alone. Scott does not hide anything in his writings; his hopes are that his writings will be a light to empathetically and affectively help others.

* 9 7 8 0 6 1 5 9 1 7 1 0